Amish & Mennonite Apple Recipes

by Kathy Yoder

©Kathy Yoder 2003

All rights reserved. No part of this book may be reproduced or transmitted in any form or by any means, electronic or mechanical, except by a reviewer who may quote brief passages in a review to be printed in a magazine or newspaper.

Reprinted in 2004, 2005, 2007, 2008, 2011, 2012, 2013 2015 and 2016.

HEARTS & TUMMIES COOKBOOK COMPANY
3544 Blakslee Street
Wever, IA 52658
800-571-2665

APPLES ARE TEMPTING!

Apple trees have the prettiest blossoms. The flowers are a fanfare. They announce loudly, in sight and smell, the upcoming arrival of the delicious fruit we call "apple." Is it any wonder that the sight, the smell, and the taste of the apple tempted Eve? I know that I can hardly pass an apple tree without thinking about all the tasty dishes my family and friends will make with this wonderful fruit. Pretty soon, I find myself just like Eve, munching on an apple and not knowing how it even got into my hand. Maybe it's good Eve didn't know about applesauce.

This humble little cookbook
is dedicated
to
Cousin Emma.
Thanks for being the sister I never had
and the friend I will always cherish.
Thanks for letting me
tell your story.

TABLE OF CONTENTS

Apple Butter, Dips, Leather & More.............9

Apples for Breakfast 17

Apple Drinks & Soup 27

Apple Muffins & Breads.......................37

Apple Salads & Vegetables 51

Apple Main Dishes.............................69

Apple Crisps, Cobblers & Crunches.......87

Apple Cookies & Bars 97

Apple Cakes 109

Apple Pies.....................................127

Apple Desserts................................149

Apple Butter, Dips, Leather & More

Apple Leather..**11**
Dried Apples **13**
Caramel Dip for Apples **14**
Cousin Emma's Apple Butter........................... **15**
Cousin Emma's Apple Pie in a Jar **16**

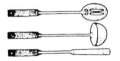

Apple Leather

Pick as many fresh apples as you like. Peel them and cut them in half.

Cover the bottom of buttered pie pans with the apple halves. Use a potato masher to pound and flatten each half.

Dry in the sun one whole day, or in a 200-degree oven for 4 to 6 hours.

For leisure chewing.

Husband David delights in my flower gardens. He doesn't say it out loud, but I see him breathing in the aroma of the lily of the valley, the purple lilac bushes or the heirloom roses that climb an old, weathered trellis next to the horse barn. I've seen him admire the pinks and the fever few. I've caught him eyeing the columbine and the cosmos.

Many of our flowers have been growing here long before we were married. The bridal wreath, which surrounds our house, has been sweetly announcing spring's arrival for more than 40 years. In fact, Husband David once said that all he has to do to know which season it is, is to stick his head out the door and inhale deeply. Ah, the sweet smell of life.

Dried Apples

**Any type of apple in any amount
Drying cloth**

Peel and slice apples. Arrange them on the cloth so that no pieces overlap. Place a fan aimed right at the apples. Turn the fan on and leave for one night. Continue drying near heat. Store in jars.

Caramel Dip for Apples

1 stick margarine
1/2 C. sugar
1 tsp. vanilla
1 can (14 oz.) sweetened, condensed milk

1 C. brown sugar
1/2 C. white corn syrup

Combine margarine, sugars and corn syrup in saucepan and heat over medium heat until melted, but not boiling. Add sweetened condensed milk and vanilla. Resume cooking, stirring constantly until mixture reaches the point of boiling. Cool, serve with apple slices.

Cousin Emma's Apple Butter

10 lbs. of uncooked apples or 5 quarts of apple sauce

1/2 C. vinegar   **4 lbs. sugar**

Mix in a large roaster and boil in the oven for 2 hours. Stir occasionally. Put in jars and seal.

Cousin Emma is so good at everything she does. I once asked her how she got to be so perfect. Was she born that way or did she grow into perfection? She just laughed at me and said she loves my sense of humor. Now, isn't that just the perfect response?

15

Cousin Emma's Apple Pie in a Jar

Syrup:

1 tsp. salt
10 C. water
1/4 tsp. nutmeg
1 C. cornstarch

4 1/2 C. sugar
2 tsp. cinnamon
3 T. lemon juice

Peel and slice enough apples for cups. Fill quart jars with tightly packed apples. Cook Cook syrup until thick and bubbly. Add the lemon juice. Pour over apples in jars. Process 20 minutes in boiling water.

Apples for Breakfast

Baked Apple Oatmeal.....................................19
Homemade Pancakes.................................... 20
Cinnamon Apple Syrup.................................21
Cousin Lydia's Homemade Waffles..... 23
Apple Fritters................................. 24
Homemade Pork Sausage with Apples...............25
Apple Sausage Breakfast Ring................ 26

Baked Apple Oatmeal

1 C. oatmeal	2 eggs, beaten
3 apples sliced & cooked	1/2 C. melted butter

Mix together and add:

1 tsp. salt	3 C. oatmeal
	2 tsp. baking powder
	1 C. milk

Blend and pour into greased 13x9-inch glass pan. Bake at 350 degrees for 30 minutes.

The amount of cooked apples you add to this depends on how apple-ly you like your dishes. The apples are a tasty addition, no matter how few or how many you use.

19

Homemade Pancakes

2 1/4 C. flour
1 tsp. salt
3 T. baking powder
A few pinches of cinnamon

2 eggs
5 T. salad oil
2 C. milk
1/2 C. sugar

Mix the dry ingredients first, then add the wet ones. Fry on a hot griddle.

These pancakes taste great with homemade Apple Butter on top. Also, try some of my Cinnamon Apple Syrup.

Cinnamon Apple Syrup

2 C. sugar	1 C. water
1/2 lb. cinnamon candy	1/4 C. vinegar

Sweet apples

Mix all the ingredients together. Place them in a saucepan.
Boil until the apples are tender.

Use as many apples as you like. I never count them out or
weigh them. I just wash and cube them. Sometimes I peel them
and sometimes I don't.

This syrup is really delicious on pancakes, French toast and waffles. And, I must admit, also on ice cream. It seems as though whenever I'm making a big batch of this, Cousin Emma finds her way to my kitchen door. I'm not exaggerating. In fact, if I'm lonely for her company, I start making this recipe.

"Are you psychic, Cousin Emma?" I joked with her the last time I saw her coming through the kitchen door.

"No, Cousin Kathy. But my nose is!"

Cousin Lydia's Homemade Waffles

3 eggs, separated	3 C. buttermilk
1/4 tsp. salt	3 C. flour
3 tsp. baking powder	3-4 T. melted butter
1 T. sugar	pinch nutmeg

Mix all of the ingredients together. Beat the egg whites until they're stiff. Fold them into the other ingredients. Pour the batter into a waffle maker.

Cousin Lydia's husband, Marvin, says that the good Lord blessed us with a day of rest. He also says that the very blessed get to eat Lydia's waffles. He's happy to count himself as one of the latter.

Apple Fritters

1 1/2 C. flour	3/4 C. milk
1 T. sugar	1 T. hot salad oil
1 T. baking powder	2 beaten eggs
3 C. apples, chopped & peeled	powdered sugar

Combine dry ingredients. Add eggs, milk, salad oil and apples. Stir until moistened. Drop batter by teaspoonful into 1/2 inches of hot oil. Cook until brown, 3-4 minutes on each side. Drain and roll in powdered sugar.

Makes about 3 dozen.

Homemade Pork Sausage with Apples

2 pounds pork cut into 1" squares	2 T. dried sage, crumbled
1 lb. pork fat, cut into 1" squares	1 tsp. salt
1/4 tsp. cayenne pepper	1/4 tsp. pepper
1 C. peeled, cored apples	

Use the medium blade on a meat grinder and grind pork coarsely. Add the rest of the ingredients and mix well. Grind again. Do not process too finely.

Shape into patties and cook over low heat until browned on both sides and cooked through.

Apple Sausage Breakfast Ring

2 lb. bulk sausage

1 1/2 C. crushed butter crackers

1/2 C. minced onion

2 large eggs

1 grated apple, peeled

1/4 C. milk

Combine all ingredients. Mix well and press in a ring mold lined with waxed paper. Chill overnight. Unmold. Remove paper. Place onto a baking sheet with raised edges.

Bake at 300 degrees for 1 hour. Sometimes I fill the center of the ring with scrambled eggs right before serving.

Apple Drinks & Soups

Cousin Emma's Hot Spiced Apple Juice............29
Cheraine's Apple Tea Cooler...........................31
Cider Punch...32
Red Hot Apple Drink......................................33
Cousin Emma's Apple Soup..............................34
Cheraine's Fruit Soup.....................................35

Cousin Emma's Hot Spiced Apple Juice

8 small apples	2 T. butter, melted
1/2 C. firmly packed brown sugar	2 whole nutmegs
4 cinnamon sticks	1/3 C. sugar
16 whole cloves	16 whole allspice
2 quarts apple juice or cider	

Core apples and remove skin from the top 1/3 of each apple. Place in baking pan. Brush with butter and sprinkle with sugar. Roast in a 350-degree oven 30-45 minutes until tender. The baking time with depend on the size and the variety of apple.

In a large saucepan, combine apple juice or cider and brown sugar. Tie spices in cheesecloth bag, crush with hammer and add to the saucepan. Bring to a boil. Cover and reduce heat. Simmer 15 minutes. Remove the spice bag and throw it away.

To serve, pour hot spiced apple juice into a large bowl. Float hot, roasted apples on the surface. Ladle into mugs and top each serving with a roasted apple. Or leave apples in the bowl until the apple juice is finished. Then place the apples in a bowl to be eaten like a dessert. Very good with ice cream.

Cousin Emma is well known for her spicy drink. Recently at a barn raising, I saw Caleb Miller drinking more then his share of this recipe. He didn't seem to want to share at all. That's not like him.

Cheraine's Apple Tea Cooler

1/3 C. apple juice, unsweetened
1/3 C. tea
Ice cubes
Lemon wedge

Mix apple juice and tea. Serve over ice cubes. Garnish with a lemon wedge if desired. This makes one serving.

Cider Punch

1 quart light corn syrup
1 gallon apple cider or apple juice
1 can (46 ounces) pineapple juice
1 can (6 ounces) frozen lemonade juice

Mix together corn syrup, pineapple juice, cider and lemonade concentrate in a large kettle.

Bring the mixture to a boil. Serve hot, or chill and serve over ice cubes. Makes 32 serves.

Red Hot Apple Drink

1/2 C. red hot cinnamon candies
Apple juice to make 30 cups

Over a medium high flame, heat apple juice in large pot on stove. Add red hot cinnamon candies. Stir constantly until candies are completely dissolved and apple juice is hot. Serve warm.

This tastes especially good after being outside in cold weather. When Husband David and Son Ethan come in after a winter morning of chores, this warms them right up. It even helps to melt Husband David's frosty beard.

Cousin Emma's Apple Soup

4 apples, pared & sliced
Zest of 1 lemon
1/2 C. apple juice
2 T. flour
1/2 C. heavy cream

1/2 C. sugar
3 C. water
1 T. butter
2 T. cold water

Combine the apples, sugar, lemon and water in a saucepan. Cook for 25 minutes over medium heat. Add apple juice. Make a "gravy" with butter, water. Thin with a little soup if necessary. Blend into soup to thicken. Simmer 5 minutes. Add heavy cream just before serving.

Cheraine's Fruit Soup

3/4 C. pitted prunes	3/4 C. dried apricots
1 stick cinnamon (about 2" long)	1 C. peeled, diced apples
6 C. cold water	1/4 C. raisins
1 C. sugar	1/4 C. quick-cooking tapioca
1/4 C. currants	
3 lemon slices	

In a medium-size saucepan, soak prunes and apricots in 6 C. water for 30 minutes. Add sugar, tapioca, lemon slices and cinnamon stick. Bring to a boil & simmer for 10 minutes. Add apples, raisins, currants. Simmer for 10 minutes more.

Cheraine is my English friend. I've known her about eight years now. We ran into each other at an auction. We were eyeing the same items. Somehow, we struck up a conversation and have been talking ever since. (Non-stop, say our husbands.)

Cheraine has a jovial laugh and a kind heart. She will do practically anything for anyone. In fact, she is so kind that she has a hard time saying "no." I think there is a special place in Heaven for her. She thinks of others before herself. Cheraine truly walks in Jesus' footsteps. She is an inspiration to me. As if that isn't enough, Cheraine also has a Scandinavian friend. That's where she got her fruit soup recipe.

Apple Muffins & Breads

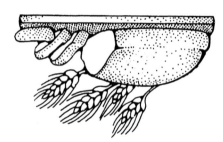

Suzanne's Spicy Apple Muffins 39
Apple-Molasses Muffins 41
Walnut Cheddar Apple Bread 45
Applesauce Fruit Bread......................... 47
Apple Pie Bread............................... 48
Applesauce Gingerbread........................ 49

Suzanne's Spicy Apple Muffins

2 C. unsifted flour	1/4 C. sugar
3 tsp. baking powder	1 tsp. pumpkin pie spice
1/2 tsp. salt	2 eggs, beaten
1/4 C. butter	1/2 C. milk
1 C. chopped apples	

Stir together flour, baking powder, sugar and salt in medium bowl. Combine eggs and remaining ingredients. Add all at once to the flour mixture. Mix only until flour is moistened and still lumpy. Drop by spoonfuls into lightly greased muffin pans. Bake at 400 degrees for 25 minutes. Makes 12 muffins.

God has richly blessed me with so many wonderful friends. They remind me of apples on a tree. From a distance they all look alike, but when you get closer, you see that no two are the same.

Suzanne is unique. She's like her recipe — spicy, never bland. She loves life and is not afraid to show it. Her enthusiasm is contagious. You can't be in a bad mood around her. She loves children. She's interested in every one she meets. She watches them grow and never forgets what makes each one of them special. She's that way with her friends, too. She never measures her affection. She pours out kindness and love to all of us. It never seems to end.

If friendship was a flavor, this friendship would be spicy.

Apple-Molasses Muffins

2 C. flour		1/4 C. sugar	
1 T. baking powder		1 tsp. cinnamon	
1/4 tsp. salt		1/2 C. milk	
1/4 C. molasses		1/4 C. vegetable oil	
1 apple peeled, cored & finely chopped			

Heat oven to 450 degrees. Lightly grease eight 3-inch muffin pan cups.

In large bowl combine flour, sugar, baking powder, cinnamon & salt. Add apple and stir so apple is distributed evenly.

(continued)

In a small bowl, beat together molasses, milk, oil, and egg. Stir into dry ingredients and mix just until blended.

Fill muffin pan cups with batter. Bake 5 minutes and then reduce heat to 350 degrees. Bake 12-15 minutes longer or until centers of muffins spring back when gently pressed.

Cool in pan 5 minutes. Remove muffins from pan. Cool slightly. Serve.

Cousin Emma has never married. She lives with her brother Jacob and his family. Her nieces and nephews, all eight of them, love her dearly. She is truly like a second mother to them, even though they have a wonderful mother in Jacob's wife, Ruth. I know that Ruth loves Emma like a sister. I've heard her say time and time again that she didn't know what she'd do without Emma. Everyone knows that she'll never find out.

I'm more likely to see a chorus of frogs flying over my house as I am to see Cousin Emma married. It's rare in an Amish community, but sometimes a woman just isn't meant to marry. That must be true with Cousin Emma. She had many interested suitors when she was young, but she just ignored them.

Once, there was a wonderful boy, Aaron, who was quite taken with Cousin Emma. He was well established on his family farm. He'd be a good provider for some lucky girl. But she told me that he would never do.

"I know this sounds silly, Cousin Kathy, but I just have to marry someone who will take me fishing."

"Can't you just ask Aaron to take you?" I asked her.

"It's just not the same." I had no idea what she was talking about, but evidentially no one else ever asked her to go fishing either.

Walnut Cheddar Apple Bread

1/2 C. butter, softened	1 C. packed brown sugar
2 eggs	1 tsp. vanilla
2 C. flour	2 tsp. baking powder
1 tsp. baking soda	1/4 tsp. salt
1 C. sour cream	1/4 C. sour milk
1 C. shredded cheddar cheese	1 C. diced, dried apple
1/2 C. coarsely chopped walnuts	

Preheat oven to 350 degrees. Grease a 9x5 loaf pan. Beat butter and sugar together until light and fluffy. Beat in eggs and vanilla until blended.

(continued)

Combine flour, baking powder, baking soda and salt in a small bowl. Add flour mixture to butter mixture and mix alternately with sour cream and milk, beginning and ending with the flour mixture. Mix well after each addition. Stir in cheese, apple and walnuts until blended. Spoon into prepared pan.

Bake 50-55 minutes. Cool in pan 15 minutes. Remove from pan and cool completely on wire rack. Store tightly wrapped in plastic wrap at room temperature.

Applesauce Fruit Bread

1 1/2 C. flour	1 C. applesauce
1/2 C. brown sugar	1/3 C. cooking oil
2 eggs	1 1/2 tsp. salt
1 tsp. baking soda	1 tsp. baking powder
1 tsp. cinnamon	1 1/2 C. quick oats
1 C. raisins	1/2 C. candied fruit

Mix together flour, applesauce, brown sugar, oil, eggs, salt, baking soda, baking powder and cinnamon until well blended. Stir in oats, raisins and candied fruits. Spoon into greased 9x5 loaf pan. Bake at 350 degrees for 1 hour or until inserted toothpick comes out clean.

Apple Pie Bread

2 C. sugar
1/2 C. oil
1 tsp. vanilla
1 T. apple pie spice
3 C. flour
3 C. finely chopped apple

1 tsp. salt
1 tsp. baking soda
1/2 C. butter
3 eggs
1 C. walnuts

Combine sugar, oil, butter and eggs, Beat well. Sift together flour, salt, spices and soda. Add to creamed mixture. Mix in vanilla, apples and walnuts. Place in two greased loaf pans. Bake at 325 degrees for 1 hour.

Applesauce Gingerbread

1 1/2 C. flour	1/8 tsp. salt
1/2 tsp. baking powder	1/2 tsp. baking soda
1 tsp. cinnamon	3/4 tsp. ginger
1 1/2 C. applesauce, divided	2 egg whites
1/2 C. molasses	1/3 C. boiling water
3 T. sugar	2 tsp. cornstarch
1/2 C. cranberry juice	whipped topping
1/3 C. firmly packed brown sugar	

Combine flour, salt, baking powder, soda, cinnamon and ginger. Set aside.

(continued)

Beat together brown sugar, 1/2 C. applesauce, egg whites & molasses until thoroughly combined. Add dry ingredients alternately with water. Spread evenly in round 9-inch greased cake pan. Bake in 350-degree oven for about 30 minutes or until toothpick inserted comes out clean. Cool.

Sauce: In saucepan, mix sugar and cornstarch. Add remaining 1 C. applesauce and juice. Cook over medium heat, stirring constantly, until it starts to boil. Reduce heat. Continue cooking and stirring 3 minutes more. Remove from heat. Cool slightly. Cut warm gingerbread in slices and serve with warm applesauce. Top with whipped topping.

Apple Salads & Vegetables

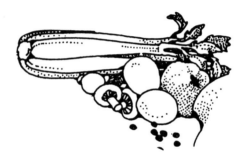

Cousin Lydia's Applesauce Ring......................53
Red Applesauce Salad 54
Cousin Lydia's Cinnamon-Apple Salad............55
Basic Apple Salad..................................59
Berry Applesauce Gelatin..........................60
Stuffed Applesauce Tomatoes.......................61
Grandma Jo's Apple Squash with Maple.........62
Apple Potato Salad..................................63
Suzanne's Spicy Apple Cole Slaw.....................64
Joe D. Annie's Red Cabbage & Apple Salad.. ..65
Apple Skillet Salad................................66

Cousin Lydia's Applesauce Ring

1 pkg. lime gelatin
1 small can crushed pineapple, drained
1/2 pint whipping cream

2 C. applesauce

Dissolve gelatin in 2 C. hot water. You may use the pineapple juice as part of the liquid. When it begins to set, whip the gelatin. Pour 1/4 of the mixture into the bottom of a mold. Red cherries may be added for color. Let set. Add the applesauce and drained pineapple to the remaining cooled gelatin. Whip cream. Fold into gelatin mixture and pour into mold.

Red Applesauce Salad

2 C. boiling water
2 3-oz. pkgs. cherry gelatin

4 C. applesauce
1/4 C. red hot candies

Dissolve red hots in boiling water. Add cherry gelatin, stirring until dissolved. Add applesauce. Pour into dish and refrigerate.

Cousin Lydia's Cinnamon-Apple Salad

6 apples, cored, peeled, cut in half   4 C. water
2 3-oz. pkgs. cream cheese, softened   1/2 C. chopped nuts
1/2 C. sugar   1/4 C. sour cream
1 stick cinnamon 3" long   1 T. fresh lemon juice
6-8 drops red food coloring

Prepare apples. In a large saucepan, mix water and sugar. Add cinnamon stick and food coloring. Bring to a boil. Simmer 10 minutes. Add apples and bring to a simmer. Baste often so apples will absorb color and flavor. Simmer for 10-15 minutes until apples are cooked through but still have their shape.

(continued)

Let cool in the syrup. remove and chill. Reserve the syrup in which apples were cooked.

Mix cream cheese, 1/4 C. chopped nuts, sour cream and lemon juice until well blended. Roll into 12 balls. Roll each ball in reserved chopped nuts and place on each apple half.

Reduce syrup in which apples were cooked until about 3/4 C. remains. Cool and spoon 1 T. over each apple half.

Dating customs are different with the Amish. Couples date in secret. The young man comes out later at night. Usually a girl pretends to be asleep. Her parent's go to bed. After a while, her suitor stands near her bedroom window and shines a flashlight. This is her signal that he is near. She carefully sneaks out of her bedroom and to the front door where she lets him in. They sit in the kitchen and talk.

Now if friends and/or family guess that the young man is courting, he will out and out lie to them. This is considered a white lie and in this instance is perfectly acceptable. Grandma Jo figured out that her son and I were courting almost the day it started, if not before.

She is a wise woman who knows how to read people.

When the young man finally asks the girl to marry him and she agrees, then he sends an older man, a Schteckleimann, to ask for the approval of the girl's parents. If they agree, the couple's intentions of marriage are announced in church at least two weeks before the wedding.

Husband David's family were elated that we were getting married. Not only because they said they were happy to make me part of their family. But also because everyone loves a wedding!

Basic Apple Salad

1 C. granulated sugar	1 C. water
2 T. flour	1 T. vinegar
1 T. butter	2 eggs
4-6 C. sliced apples	

Mix all the ingredients, except the apples, into a saucepan. Cook until thick. Pour over the apples. Serve warm or cold.

Berry Applesauce Gelatin

1 6 oz. package strawberry gelatin
1 C. boiling water
2 C. frozen unsweetened strawberries
2 C. applesauce

2 T. lemon juice

In a bowl, dissolve gelatin in boiling water. Stir in the strawberries until thawed and separated. Add the applesauce and lemon juice. Mix well. Pour into an 11x7x2-inch pan. Chill until set.

Stuffed Applesauce Tomatoes

8 medium tomatoes	2 1/2 T. butter
2/3 C. finely chopped onion	2/3 C. dry bread crumbs
1 1/4 C. applesauce	1/2 tsp. sage
1/3 C. grated parmesan cheese	
3/4 tsp. salt	dash of pepper

Wash tomatoes thoroughly. Cut a slice from the top of each tomato. Carefully scoop out the centers. Sauté onion in butter until lightly browned. Add bread crumbs, applesauce, sage, salt, and pepper. Place filling in tomatoes. Sprinkle with grated parmesan cheese. Bake 350 degrees for 25-30 minutes.

Grandma Jo's Apple Squash with Maple

2 C. applesauce
1/4 C. maple sugar, crushed
2 C. smoothly mashed winter squash
1/3 C. evaporated milk

1/2 tsp. salt
pinch of pepper
1/4 C. melted butter
1 C. dry bread crumbs

Combine applesauce and squash, then blend in maple sugar, salt, pepper and 1 T. of the melted butter. Add the milk. Stir until well mixed. Pour into greased 1 1/2 quart casserole. Combine remaining melted margarine with the crumbs and spread evenly over surface of mixture in casserole. Bake in 375 oven for about 45 minutes.

Apple Potato Salad

5 C. cooked potato, cubed	1 1/2 C. apple, diced
1/2 C. green pepper, chopped	1 C. plain, nonfat yogurt
1/4 C. onion, chopped	1/2 C. mayonnaise

In large bowl, combine potatoes, apple dices, green pepper and onion. Toss lightly with a mixture of yogurt and mayonnaise. Serve on lettuce if desired.

Suzanne's Spicy Apple Cole Slaw

1/3 C. mayonnaise
1 tsp. grated orange rind
A pinch of cinnamon, ground cloves & salt
6 C. shredded cabbage
2 C. apples, shredded

1/4 C. sour cream
1 T. orange juice

1 T. sugar

Combine mayonnaise, sour cream, orange juice, and grated rind. Add salt, spices & sugar. Mix thoroughly. Pour over the cabbage. Mix gently but thoroughly. Cover the bowl and chill. Just before serving, toss the apple lightly with the cabbage.

Joe D. Annie's Red Cabbage & Apple Salad

1 qt. shredded red cabbage	1 tsp. salt
2 T brown sugar	3 T butter
1/2 t mustard	2 T. vinegar
1/2 C. sour cream pepper	1 C. apples quartered & sliced

Melt the butter in a saucepan. Add the cabbage and apple. Stir until the butter coats the mixture and there are signs of softening, but the mixture is not really cooked. Add the vinegar, sugar, seasonings and mustard. Simmer another 2 minutes then stir in the sour cream. Serve hot.

Apple Skillet Salad

4 slices bacon
1/4 C. vinegar
1 C. diced apples
1/2 C. chopped parsley

1 T. onion, chopped
4 C. shredded cabbage
1 T. brown sugar
1 tsp. salt

Cook the bacon until crisp. Remove from skillet and crumble. Add vinegar, sugar, salt, onion and apple to bacon fat. Heat thoroughly. Remove from the stove. Toss the cabbage and parsley in the hot dressing.

Husband David is a tall man. I never set out to marry someone so tall. When I first met him he was sitting down. From that angle he looked about average in height. In fact, everything about him seemed average, except for his blonde hair, the color of fresh straw in the summer sun. But things like that never turned my head. Well, not much. What turned my head was his laughter.

His is not a reserved chuckle or even a galloping guffaw. It's an unbridled explosion of sound. When I first heard that sound, my heart stopped, for just a second. I was in the process of walking past him. It seemed a little forward, but I turned around and looked him straight in the eyes. Some might have thought I was being flirtatious. I wasn't. I was taking his measure.

I wanted to see if there was laughter in his eyes. Have you ever noticed that some people make a laughing sound, but their eyes are serious? It means that they aren't really laughing from deep down in their souls. They're just surface laughing. They're laughing to be polite. They're laughing because it's to their advantage. They're laughing because everyone else is laughing. And sometimes that kind of laughter is short.

But Husband David's laughter was honest laughter, filled with warmth and joy. He still laughs that way today, a long, tall laugh. And I laugh with him.

Apple Main Dishes

Apple-Stuffed Acorn Squash............................... 71
Chicken & Rice Salad with Apples 75
Yam & Apple Casserole.................................77
Pork Chops with Applesauce Gravy 79
Sausages with Baked Apples 80
Magdalena's Baked Apple Dumplings............. 81
Sarah's Surprise Apple Dumplings 83
Boiled Apple Dumplings 85

Apple-Stuffed Acorn Squash

3 acorn squash	3 tart, red apples
1/2 C. maple syrup	1/4 C. butter, melted
1 C. broken cashew nuts	

Wash squash. Cut in half lengthwise. Scoop out seeds and stringy material. Wash, core and dice unpared apples. Combine with remaining ingredients.

Fill squash halves with apple mixture. Brush surface with additional melted butter. Put in baking dish and pour boiling water in dish 1/2" deep.

(continued)

Cover dish with foil. Bake in a preheated 400-degree oven for 45 minutes. Uncover and bake an additional 10 minutes. Test the squash with a fork to make sure it's tender.

This sounds like a lot of work, but it really isn't. It tastes so good with a beef roast, homemade dinner rolls, cinnamon apple salad and, of course, an apple pie topped off with homemade ice cream.

It's a wonderful "Salute to Autumn" meal.

5 Something strange happened the other day. I saw Cousin Emma in town taking to Caleb Miller. I know that sounds innocent enough, but Cousin Emma's face was an unusual shade of red. That always means trouble.

One time I remember seeing her face that color was when we were little and got caught in her father's barn. We were dressing a lamb in some of Cousin Emma's old clothes. They didn't fit her any more and we thought it would be fun to see how the lamb looked in Amish dress. Her father was not amused. Cousin Emma's face was bright red when her Da said she should go inside and do something useful instead of ruining perfectly good clothes.

Or the time Cousin Emma and I were at a church meeting. The boys sit up front with the men and the girls sit in the back with the women. Cousin Emma started giggling. Her face turned bright red. She got stern looks from both sides of the room.

It wasn't really her fault. Someone had dropped a tiny frog on her lap as they walked by. She didn't notice it at first. When she did, she didn't scream like most girls would. Cousin Emma has always loved insects and frogs and animals.

So, instead of screaming, she laughed right out loud. When she realized that everyone was looking at her, she bent her head down. Her face was red. Come to think of it, Caleb Miller had walked by us right before Cousin Emma saw the frog.

Chicken & Rice Salad with Apples

4 Golden Delicious Apples	4 T. lemon juice
1 lb. boned, cooked chicken, cubed (4 cups)	
1 1/4 C. shelled, fresh green peas, blanched	
1 1/4 C. mayonnaise	2 1/2 T. milk
1/2 C. minced parsley	2 tsp. Dijon mustard
1 tsp. celery seed	1/2 tsp. pepper
1/2 C. green onions thinly sliced	3 C. cooled cooked rice
4 heads of lettuce or other greens	

Core but do not peel apples. Dice them into a medium bowl.

(continued)

Add lemon juice. Toss well. Add mayonnaise, milk, mustard, celery seed and pepper. Mix well. Set aside.

In a large bowl combine rice, chicken, peas, parsley and green onions. mix well. Add apple mixture and mix thoroughly. Cover and chill until ready to serve. Spoon salad onto salad greens.

Serve chilled or room temperature. Makes 16 servings.

Yam & Apple Casserole

4 large yams	1 T. fresh lemon juice
3 large cooking apples	2 C. hot apple juice
3 T. butter	1/2 tsp. ground allspice
1/2 tsp. ground cinnamon	1 T. cornstarch
1/2 C. firmly packed brown sugar	1/2 C. raisins

Parboil the yams for 40 minutes. Peel and slice 1/3" thick. Peel, core and thinly slice apples. In a small pan melt butter. Add cornstarch and sugar. Mix in lemon juice, hot apple juice, allspice and cinnamon. Continue cooking for 5-6 minutes.

(continued)

In a shallow greased casserole dish, alternate layers of sliced yams and apples. Sprinkle raisins over the top. Pour over the hot apple juice mixture.

Cover with foil and bake in a preheated 375-degree oven for one hour. Remove foil and continue baking for an additional 30 minutes, basting frequently.

Pork Chops with Applesauce Gravy

2 C. applesauce	3 lbs. pork chops
1 T. minced garlic	1/2 C. flour
1 T. salt	1/8 tsp. pepper
3 C. boiling water	1 T. lemon juice

Brown pork chops in frying pan. Remove to 3-quart casserole dish. Brown the garlic in the remaining fat. Add flour, salt and pepper. Blend. Add water. Cook until the mixture thickens, stirring constantly. Add applesauce and lemon juice. Stir. Pour over pork chops. Bake at 425 degrees until tender (about 1 1/2 hours). Serves 8.

Sausages with Baked Apples

1 lb. sausages   4 large, tart apples

Use either sausages or sausage meat. Cook sausages, remove from fat and keep warm while cooking the apples.

Cut the apples in 1/4-inch slices, leaving the skin on. Fry in the sausage fat until the apples are soft, but not broken.

Serve sausages on a hot platter, surrounded with the apples. Serves 6.

Magdalena's Baked Apple Dumplings

Pastry for double crust pie	cinnamon
3 large baking apples	3 T. butter
Milk	6 tsp. sugar

Roll out 3/4 of the pastry as you would for pies. Cut into fourths, as you would cut a pie. Pare, core apples and cut in half. Place an apple half on each section of pastry, cut side up. Over each apple put 1 tsp. sugar, a dash of cinnamon, and 1/2 T. butter. Bring up edges of of dough around apple, but leave opening for steam to escape. Cut off extra corners of dough and add to unused pastry. Place dumplings in baking dish. Roll out rest of dough and make other dumplings. Bake in a 350-degree oven for 20-30 minutes.

Magdalena is getting quite elderly, but she still outcooks most the women half her age. She can stand for hours over a hot stove and not utter a complaint. I once saw her do this all day when she was cooking for her oldest granddaughter's wedding.

"Magdalena, how can you do this and not get stiff and sore? Or at least tired?" I asked her.

"I don't have time. I'm praying love into each one of these dishes. And I'm praying that Elizabeth and Ben have a happy and long marriage. I pray for every child, every grandchild and every great-grandchild every day. I let God take care of the rest."

Sarah's Surprise Apple Dumplings

Crust for 4 Dumplings:
Sift 1 1/2 C. flour with 3/4 tsp. salt. Cut in 1/2 C. shortening.
Gradually add 3 or 4 T. cold milk. Toss lightly until ingredients
are moistened. Chill.

Syrup:

2/3 C. sugar	1/4 tsp. cinnamon
1 C. water	2 T. butter
A few drops of red food coloring	

Boil together about 3 minutes.

Surprise Filling:

Brown sugar & nuts
Prepared mincemeat
Dates, nuts & honey

Your favorite jelly
Raisins & honey
Brown sugar & coconut

Roll crust into a 14" square. Cut into 4-7" squares. Place a peeled, cored, tart baking apple on each. Fill with surprise fillings, sprinkle with sugar & dot with butter. Fold up corners of the crust over the top of the apple. Pinch crust edges together. Place the dumplings in a deep baking dish. Add syrup. Bake at 400 degrees for 40-45 minutes or until apple is tender. Serve warm with cream or ice cream.

Boiled Apple Dumplings

2 C. flour	3/4 C. milk
4 tsp. baking powder	3 large tart apples
1/2 tsp. salt	6 tsp. sugar
2 T. sugar	milk
2 T. shortening	

Sift together flour, baking powder, salt & sugar. Stir in milk. On floured board, roll dough to 1/2-inch thickness. Cut into 6 squares.

Pare & core apples. Cut in halves. Put a half on each square of dough & 1 tsp. sugar on each apple.

85

Pull the four corners of the dough together, dampen slightly and press to seal. Tie each dumpling in a clean piece of white muslin. Drop dumplings in a large kettle of boiling water. Cook 20-25 minutes, depending upon the size of the apples. Serve in bowls with milk and additional sugar if needed.

Husband David loves this dish. In fact, when he gets a craving for it, he doesn't just ask me to make it for him. He has another way of hinting. He calls me his little dumpling. I'm not sure that's a compliment. He says he likes my dimples when I smile and my dumplings when he's hungry. Men. Who can understand them?

Apple Crisps, Cobblers & Crunches

Jean's Apple Crisp..89
Joe D. Annie's Apple-Pear Cobbler...................91
Vanilla-Scented Biscuit Topping.......................93
Oma's Apple Crunch...95
Apple Crisp for Two, or 1 Hungry Boy.............96

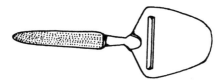

Jean's Apple Crisp

4 C. peeled, chopped apples	2/3 C. brown sugar
1/2 C. oats	3/4 tsp. nutmeg
1/2 C. flour	3/4 tsp. cinnamon
1/3 C. butter	

Arrange apples in an 8x8x2 greased pan.

Mix other ingredients and sprinkle over apples.

Bake at 375 degrees until apples are tender, about 30 minutes.
Nuts can also be sprinkled on top.

Friend Jean and I have a shared vice. It's coffee. Well, sometimes it's hot chocolate and it's also been lemonade and even tea. I guess it depends on the season. Mainly, we love to get together and chat.

I don't remember what we talk about. We're both so busy with every day life that we don't get together as much as we'd like. Some day, when our laundry loads are lighter and our children are happily married and we don't have to worry about them, we'll have more time for our vice. In the meantime, we sip our drinks slowly. By the time we hit the bottom of the cup or glass, It's time to get busy again. Whatever we talk about makes my step lighter, my path straighter and my smile wider.

Joe D. Annie's Apple-Pear Cobbler

3 cooking apples, peeled, cored & sliced

2 T. unsalted butter, melted & cooled

3 pears, peeled, cored & sliced   **1 tsp. lemon juice**

1/4 C. apple butter blended with **1/4 C. apple cider**
and **3 T. sugar**

1 recipe Vanilla Scented Biscuit Topping

Preheat the oven to 425 degrees. Butter a 9- to 10-inch oval oven-proof baking dish that is 3 inches deep.

In a mixing bowl, toss the apples and pears with the lemon juice and apple butter, apple cider and sugar blend.

Let stand for 5 minutes. Spoon the fruit into the baking dish. Drizzle the butter over the fruit.

Drop heaping tablespoons of the biscuit topping over the fruit. Bake the cobbler for 10 minutes. Reduce the oven temperature to 400 degrees and continue baking for about 35 minutes longer, or until the fruit is tender and the topping is golden.

Vanilla-Scented Biscuit Topping

1 1/2 cups all-purpose flour	2 tsp. baking powder
1/8 tsp. salt	3/4 tsp.ground cinnamon
1/4 tsp. nutmeg	1/8 tsp. ground allspice
3 T. cold, unsalted butter, cubed	3 T. shortening
2 T. sugar	3/4 C. milk
1 1/2 tsp. vanilla extract	

In a large bowl whisk together the flour, baking powder, salt, cinnamon, nutmeg and allspice. Using a pastry blender or two knives, cut in the butter and shortening until mixture resembles coarse crumbs. Mix in the sugar.

(continued)

In a small bowl, mix the milk with the vanilla extract. Stir the milk mixture into the flour mixture until blended and the dough is medium-firm and sticky. When scooped with a spoon, it should hold its shape.

Use biscuit dough as directed in Joe D. Annie's Apple-Pear Cobbler recipe. Serves 6.

Oma's Apple Crunch

5-6 medium apples	1/4 C. sugar
1/2 tsp. cinnamon	1/2 tsp. nutmeg
1/2 C. soft butter	1/2 C. brown sugar
1 C. flour	1/2 tsp. salt

Peel & slice apples. Cover bottom of casserole with apple pieces. Spread sugar, cinnamon and nutmeg over apples. Mix butter, brown sugar, flour and salt together until crumbly. Spread on apples.

Bake in 350-degree oven until a light brown. Serve with milk while hot.

Apple Crisp for Two, or 1 Hungry Boy

2 apples
1 T. brown sugar
Dash of salt
1 T. butter, cut in small pieces

1 T. flour
1 tsp. cinnamon
3 tsp. water

Peel and core apples, then slice them directly onto cookie sheet. In small bowl blend flour, brown sugar, cinnamon & salt. Pour flour mixture over apples. Sprinkle water over all ingredients. Use more water if apples are not very juicy. Space out pieces of butter over top. Bake in 375-degree oven for 30 minutes.

Apple Cookies & Bars

Esther's Applesauce Cookies..............................99
Applesauce Spice Cookies..................................100
Fresh Apple Cookies..101
Barbara's Applesauce Spice Bars........................103
Barbara's Browned Butter Frosting..................104
Apple Oat Sesame Cookies..............................105
Apple Cookies..107

Esther's Applesauce Cookies

2 eggs	1/2 tsp. nutmeg
1 tsp. vanilla	1/2 tsp. salt
2 C. applesauce	1 tsp. cinnamon
1 C. whole wheat flour	1/2 C. chopped nuts
2 C. quick oats	1 C. dates, chopped
1 tsp. soda	

Mix together eggs, vanilla and applesauce. Set aside. Mix together dry ingredients. Stir in the applesauce mixture. Mix until smooth. Add dates and nuts. Drop onto cookie sheet. Bake at 325 degrees for 15-20 minutes.

Applesauce Spice Cookies

1/2 C. softened butter
1 egg
1 T. baking powder
1 tsp. cinnamon
1/2 tsp. nutmeg
1 3/4 C. quick-cooking rolled oats

1 C. sugar
1 C. flour
1/2 tsp. salt
1/2 tsp. cloves
1 C. applesauce
1 C. raisins

Beat butter & sugar together until creamy. Beat in egg. Combine the next six ingredients in separate bowl and stir into creamy mixture. Stir in applesauce, oats and raisins. Drop by teaspoon onto greased baking sheets. Bake about 15 minutes in a preheated 375 oven until lightly browned. Makes 5 dozen.

Fresh Apple Cookies

2 2/3 C. brown sugar
2 tsp. baking soda
1 tsp. salt
1 tsp. nutmeg
4 C. flour
2 C. chopped apples

Cookie Dough:
16 T. butter
2 eggs
2 tsp. ground cloves
2 tsp. cinnamon
1/2 C. apple juice
2 cups chopped nuts
2 C. raisins

Glaze:
3 C. powdered sugar
5 T. apple juice

1/4 tsp. salt
2 T. margarine

1/2 tsp. vanilla

Cream together margarine, brown sugar and eggs. Add baking soda, spices and apple juice and mix well. Gradually add flour, mixing well after each addition. Fold in apples, raisins and nuts. Drop by heaping teaspoonfuls onto lightly greased cookie sheet.

Bake at 375 degrees for 10-12 minutes. To prepare glaze combine all ingredients and beat until smooth. With a knife spread warm cookies with glaze.

Makes 5 dozen cookies.

Barbara's Applesauce Spice Bars

1 C. flour	1 tsp. soda
2/3 C. packed brown sugar	1/2 tsp. salt
1/4 C. shortening	1 C. applesauce
1 tsp. pumpkin pie spice	1 egg
1/4 C. shortening	1/2 C. raisins

Heat oven to 350 degrees. Grease a 13X9-inch pan. Mix all ingredients thoroughly. Spread in pan. Bake 25 minutes Cool and frost with Browned butter Frosting. Cut into bars.

Barbara's Browned Butter Frosting

3 T. butter
1 1/2 C. powdered sugar

1 tsp. vanilla
1 T. milk

Heat butter in saucepan until delicate brown. Blend in the remaining ingredients and beat until the frosting is smooth. Spread on cake.

Friend Barbara says that the pumpkin pie spice adds a little twist to the Applesauce Spice Bars. She also says that the regular powdered sugar frosting is good on the bars, but the cooking adds yet another little twist to the overall flavor. I don't argue with Barbara. She's well known for her baking skills.

Apple Oat Sesame Cookies

3/4 C. flour	3/4 C. flour
3/4 C. whole wheat flour	1/2 C. quick cooking oats
1/4 C. sugar	1/4 C. sesame seeds
1 tsp. baking powder	1 tsp. cinnamon
1/2 tsp. nutmeg	1/2 tsp. baking soda
1/2 C. honey	1/4 tsp. salt
1/2 C. vegetable oil	
1 large egg	1/3 C. milk
	3/4 C. raisins

1 1/2 C. finely chopped apples. Golden Delicious works well.

(continued)

Heat oven to 375 degrees. In a large bowl, mix both flours, oats, sesame seeds, sugar, cinnamon, baking powder, baking soda, nutmeg and salt. Stir in apples.

In a small bowl, beat together honey, oil, milk and egg. Add to oat mixture and stir until combined. Fold in raisins (optional). Drop by tablespoonfuls onto ungreased cookie sheets.

Bake 10-12 minutes or until lightly browned.

Apple Cookies

1 tsp. soda	1/2 C. shortening
1 tsp. cinnamon	1 1/2 C. brown sugar
1 tsp. cloves	1 egg
1/2 tsp. nutmeg	1 C. applesauce
1/2 tsp. salt	1 C. chopped nuts
2 1/2 C. flour	

Add soda and spices to the flour. Cream shortening and sugar. Add egg. Add flour mixture and applesauce alternately to sugar and shortening, add nuts last. Drop from a spoon to the baking sheet. Bake at 375 degrees for 10-14 minutes.

While still hot, frost with the following frosting:

1 1/2 C. powdered sugar
1 tsp. butter

1/2 tsp. vanilla
2 T. cream

These are Cousin Emma's favorite cookies. They're an odd choice for a favorite. They're good, but it's not like they have chocolate in them. I guess her choice reflects her personality. She has simple tastes and simple needs. But when she makes a quilt, she goes all out. That's why she's so popular at quilting bees. She has such fresh ideas and is able to implement them without offending anyone. Her family and friends' children benefit greatly from her talent. She makes them all double ring wedding quilts for their wedding day.

Apple Cakes

Apple Angel Cake 111
Apple Pudding Cake 113
Mother's Applesauce 114
Applesauce Cake...117
Cousin Lydia's Apple Butter Spice Cake 119
Apple Scripture Cake 121
Apple Nut Coffee Cake.. 123

Apple Angel Cake

1 1/4 C. sifted powdered sugar	1 C. sifted cake flour
2 T. dried, crushed apple geranium leaves	

Sift all three ingredients together three times.

1 1/2 C. egg whites	1/4 tsp. salt
1 1/2 tsp. cream of tartar	1 1/2 tsp. vanilla
1 C. granulated sugar	

Beat egg whites with cream of tartar, salt & vanilla until stiff enough to form soft peaks, but still moist and glossy.

Add granulated sugar, 2 T. at a time, continuing to beat until meringue holds stiff peaks.

Sift 1/4 of flour mixture over whites and fold in. Fold in remaining flour in fourths.

Bake in ungreased 10" tube pan about 30 minutes at 375 degrees.

The apple geranium is a special scented geranium. It's important to take the leaves off whole, let them dry and then crush them. Otherwise, the scent will disappear. Serve with hot, homemade applesauce. Chocolate mint geranium leaves are also very tasty.

Apple Pudding Cake

Cream together 1/4 C. butter, 1 beaten egg and 1 C. sugar. Add 1 C. flour, 1/2 tsp. nutmeg, a dash of salt and 1 tsp. baking soda.
Mix in 3 medium peeled and diced apples and 1/2 C. nuts. The batter will be thick. Bake for 30 minutes in a 350-degree oven.

Sauce:

1/2 C. brown sugar	1/2 C. half and half
1/2 C. sugar	1/2 C. butter
Boil until thick. Add 1 tsp. vanilla	

113

Mother's Applesauce Cake

Cream together 1 C. butter, 3 tsp. vanilla and 2 C. sugar.

Sift 4 C. flour with your choice of spices five times. Mix in 3 tsp. baking soda.

Mix together 2 1/2 C. stewed apples, 1 C. chopped nuts, 1 C. grape juice or 2 eggs and 1 C. raisins.

Add the flour mixture and the apple mixture alternately to the creamed butter and sugar. Bake in a tube pan at 350 degrees for about an hour.

I've known Cousin Emma all my life. We're both from families brimming over with boys. Now we think they're great, but back then we forged a friendship as a reaction to a life filled with too many brothers. Over the years we've grown into more than just friends, we're kindred spirits.

I used to wish that Cousin Emma was my real sister so we could spend even more time together, although our parents let us visit each other all the time. We've always been inseparable. When we were young, we shared all our secrets. As we've grown up, we're still close, but I wonder if Cousin Emma is hiding something from me.

When I mentioned seeing her in town talking to Caleb Miller, her response was, "Oh." And she looked away. I expected her to tell me that Caleb was doing some extra carpentry work for the General Store. Caleb's highly regarded for his skill by the Amish and English alike. I expected her to say that she accidentally bumped into him on the way to the fabric shop. Cousin Emma is well known for her beautiful quilts.

But instead, she changed the subject. In all these years, I've never known Cousin Emma to be evasive, especially with me. If I didn't know better, I'd think she and Caleb were courting. But that's a ridiculous notion. Cousin Emma is well past the marrying age. Everyone knows that, especially Cousin Emma. And Caleb Miller will never marry. Everyone says so.

Applesauce Cake

1 2/3 C. flour
1 tsp. soda
3/4 tsp. salt
1/2 tsp. cinnamon
1/4 tsp. double action baking powder

1 1/3 C. sugar
1/4 tsp. allspice
1/4 tsp. cloves

Sift above ingredients into a mixing bowl.

Add:

1/3 C. shortening
1 C. unsweetened applesauce
1/3 C. water

(continued)

Beat 200 strokes. Add one egg. Beat 200 strokes. Add 1/3 C. chopped nuts and 2/3 C. raisins. Mix.

Bake in buttered square or oblong pan for 50 minutes at 350 degrees.

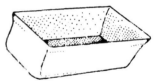

Cousin Lydia's Apple Butter Spice Cake

2 1/2 C. flour	3/4 C. apple butter
1 tsp. baking powder	2 eggs
1/2 tsp. salt	1 C. sour cream
1 C. sugar	1 tsp. vanilla
1 tsp. soda	1/2 C. butter

Put all the ingredients in a large bowl. Blend on low speed until moistened. Then blend 2 minutes on medium speed. Pour half the batter into a greased 9x13-inch cake pan. Sprinkle with half the topping. Spoon the rest of the batter on top of the topping.

(continued)

Cover with the remaining topping. Bake at 350 degrees 40-45 minutes.

Topping:

1/2 C. brown sugar	1/2 tsp. nutmeg
1 tsp. cinnamon	1/2 C. chopped nuts

Cousin Lydia says this is easier to make than not to make. At first, I had no idea what she was talking about. Then, I figured it out. Lydia feels guilty if she doesn't have a dessert freshly made every day for her family. Since this is so easy to make, she can feel like she achieved her dessert goal. She doesn't have to feel guilty for depriving her family. And, she has a little extra time to herself.

Apple Scripture Cake

1 C. vegetable oil	1/2 tsp. salt
1 1/2 C. sugar	2 tsp. cinnamon
2 eggs + 1 egg white	1 tsp. vanilla
3 large apples peeled, cored & diced	
2 C. flour	1 C. chopped nuts
1 tsp. soda	

In a large bowl, beat oil & sugar until smooth. Beat in eggs, egg white and vanilla. Stir in flour, soda, salt & cinnamon. Beat well. Stir in apples and nuts. Pour mixture into a greased 9x13 pan. Bake at 350 degrees for 45 minutes or until center springs back when gently pressed. Cool.

(continued)

Frosting:
1/2 C. softened butter
1 egg yolk

1 tsp. vanilla
1 1/2 C. powdered sugar

Beat butter in bowl. Add remaining ingredients. Beat until smooth. Spread on cooled cake.

I call this my "Apple Scripture Cake" because when I'm having trouble figuring out a Bible passage, I take a break and make this recipe. Like Eve, apples tempt me. When I first made this recipe as a child, I used to pray that it would turn out okay. It vastly improved my prayer life.

Apple Nut Coffee Cake

1/2 C. shortening	1 tsp. baking powder
1 C. sugar	1 tsp. baking soda
2 eggs	1/4 tsp. salt
1 tsp. vanilla	1 C. sour cream
2 C. flour	2 C. finely chopped apples

Cream shortening and sugar. Add eggs and vanilla. Beat well. Stir together flour, baking powder, soda and salt. Add to creamed mixture alternately with sour cream.

Fold in chopped apples. Spread batter in greased 13x9-inch baking pan.

(continued)

Combine topping ingredients and sprinkle mixture evenly over batter. Bake for 35 minutes at 350 degrees.

Topping:

1/2 C. brown sugar
2 T. melted butter
1 tsp. cinnamon
1/2 C. chopped nuts

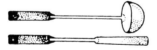

Husband David and I went for a short drive last Sunday. It was so nice to have a little time just to ourselves. As we were traveling down the road I noticed a beautiful hill filled with tall prairie grass blowing gently in the wind. In fact, the breeze was so gentle, the scene looked like it was happening in slow motion. I believe that there are times in our lives when the Lord slows life down for us. He does this for various reasons.

Sometimes, it's so that we can look at our lives and give thanks. Sometimes, it's so that we can look at our lives and ask for help. Sometimes, it's just for joy. Whatever the reason, it always seems to happen at just the right time.

Of course, God's time is always the right time, but we don't always know that until we slow down and look back. We need the perspective that time gives. Sometimes that happens in a month, a year, or a lifetime.

As we were riding down the road, I looked at that beautiful sea of prairie grass. For just a second, I thought about the pioneers coming to this part of the country. Maybe a pioneer mother, bone weary from the journey across land without roads and days without rest, maybe she glanced up for a moment. And maybe in that moment, time slowed down for her. She looked and saw this same sea of prairie grass and said, "Thanks, Lord. I needed a place to rest my eyes, my thoughts, my legs and my heart." I think I would have liked her.

Apple Pies

Magdalena's Apple Pecan Pie......................... 129
Oma's Quick Apple Cobbler Pie..................... 130
Sarah's Apple Pie Supreme............................ 133
Fresh Apple Cream Pie 134
Sue's Apple Pie 135
Oma's Crumbly Apple Pie.............................. 137
June's Fancy Caramel Nut Apple Pie 139
Pastry for 10-inch Double Crust 142
Mose Annie's Sour Cream Apple Pie 143
Grandma Yoder's Apple Pie........................... 147

Magdalena's Apple Pecan Pie

1/4 C. soft butter	1/4 tsp. salt
3/4 C. sugar	3 eggs
2 T. flour	unbaked pie shell
1 1/2 C. diced fresh apples	1/2 C. white syrup

Cream butter, sugar and flour. Stir in syrup and salt. Mix well. Beat in eggs one at a time, just until blended. Add apples. Pour into pie shell. Sprinkle with nut topping: Combine 1/4 C. flour and 1/4 C. brown sugar. Work in 2 T. soft butter until crumbly. Add 1/2 C. chopped pecans. Bake at 350 degrees for 50-60 minutes.

Oma's Quick Apple Cobbler Pie

1/4 C. flour
3/4 to 1 C. sugar
1 tsp. baking powder

1/2 C. milk
1 pt. fresh apples, cubed
3 T. butter

Sift dry ingredients into baking dish. Blend in milk and melted butter. Pour in apples, mix lightly.

Bake 400 degrees for 45 minutes or until top is brown. Serve plain or with milk or cream.

Grandma Jo loves to cook and bake with apples. She can whip up something scrumptious without even thinking about it. I remember when I was a new bride visiting her. She was chatting with me in the kitchen and the whole time she was peeling, coring, slicing and dicing apples.

"What are you making?" I asked.

"Oh, whatever seems like the right thing. It'll come to me," she smiled sweetly. As we talked more, the apples found a home in a double-crusted crumb pie. It smelled wonderful and tasted like a slice of Heaven.

131

"What kind of apples did you use?" I asked her.

"Oh. They're just windfalls a neighbor gave me."

I thought that was a special kind of apple I'd never heard of. It was a long time before I discovered that they are simply the apples that the wind has blown off the tree. They fall to the ground and lie there until someone picks them up and makes them into something special.

That's what happened to me. I was a windfall. I was a sinner who was blown off the tree of life. I lay on the ground until Jesus came and picked me up and made me into something special.

Sarah's Apple Pie Supreme

1 unbaked pie shell
5 to 6 medium apples
1/2 C. honey
3 T. flour

2 eggs
pinch salt
2 T. butter

Put eggs and salt in mixing bowl. Beat well until fluffy. Add honey and flour. Beat again. Add soft butter, beat. Pour over apples. Bake 450 degrees for 15 minutes. Then bake at 350 degrees for 45 minutes more.

Fresh Apple Cream Pie

1 unbaked pie shell
6 apples
1 C. cream
1 T. lemon juice

2 T. cornstarch
1 C. sugar
1 tsp. almond extract

Slice apples, toss with lemon juice and place into a pie crust. Mix the rest of the ingredients and pour over apples. Bake 350 degrees for 1 hour.

Please note: Don't place this on an open window sill to cool. I have found out the hard way that apple pie has a way of disappearing. I won't name names, but the guilty husband knows who he is.

Sue's Apple Pie

| 1 1/2 C. flour | 1/2 tsp. salt |
| 1/2 C. lard or shortening | 1/4 C. water |

Mix flour and salt. Blend in lard with pastry blender to the consistency of coarse meal. Add water a little at a time to make a dough that will just hold together. Mix lightly.

Turn out part of the dough onto a floured surface. Pat into a circular shape and roll. This makes enough for a double crust pie.

(continued)

Filling:

4 to 6 tart cooking apples	1 T. flour
3/4 C. sugar and cinnamon	1 T. butter

Line a pie pan with crust and fill with thinly sliced apples blended with sugar, flour and spice. Cover with top crust which has been slit to allow steam to escape. Tear a strip of cloth about an inch wide and wet it. Place the cloth around the edge of the pie. Pin in place. This keeps all the juice in the pie.

Bake in 450-degree oven for 10 minutes. Reduce heat to 375 degrees and bake for 30 minutes more.

Oma's Crumbly Apple Pie

Mix: 1/2 cup sugar and 1 teaspoon cinnamon with 4 cups apples that have been cut up for pie. Place in unbaked pie shell.

Mix: 1 cup brown sugar, 1 cup flour and 1/2 cup butter until it makes a crumbly mixture. Sprinkle mixture over apples. Bake in a 375-degree oven until apples are tender. Serve with cream.

There might be "pinches of this and pinches of that" that I can't recall. I know it was always made with pounds of love.

My Oma was the best pie baker I've ever known. In thinking back, she reminds me of a magician I saw once when I was a child. We were in town and he was performing on the street. He made a coin appear from behind my ear.

Oma never made money out of nothing, but she could take the most ordinary ingredients like flour and sugar and apples and butter and add a pinch of this and that. She'd put it in the oven and pretty soon, just like magic, the best apple pie I'd ever tasted would emerge. I've tried to recreate her pies, but the magic left the day she went to heaven. No one has made a pie smell as good or taste as good ever since.

June's Fancy Caramel-Nut Apple Pie

10-inch double crust pastry	1 T. fresh lemon juice
1/4 C. butter, softened	1/2 C. sugar
1/2 C. firmly packed brown sugar	1 T. flour
2 T. light corn syrup	1/2 tsp. cinnamon
1/2 C. pecan halves	1/2 tsp. nutmeg
1/4 tsp. cloves	
5 large, tart apples, pared, cored & thinly sliced	

Prepare pie dough and refrigerate until ready to use. Grease a 10-inch pie plate with 1 T. butter. In pan, melt the remaining 3 T. butter. Add brown sugar and corn syrup. Stir over heat only until dissolved, about 1 to 2 minutes.

139

Pour mixture in bottom of pie plate. Arrange pecan halves on plate, rounded side down. Roll out the bottom crust and carefully fit it over the top of the nut-sugar mixture.

Trim the crust even with the outer edge of the pie plate.

Sprinkle apple slices with lemon juice. In a bowl, combine sugar, flour and spices. Toss with apple slices.

Spread apple slices evenly in the pie plate, peaking slightly in center.

(continued on page 141)

(continued)

Roll out the remaining pastry and place over the apple mixture. Trim the top crust 1/2" beyond the edge of the bottom crust; tuck the top crust under the edge of bottom crust to seal. Cut slits in the top crust.

Bake in preheated 400-degree oven for 50 minutes. Remove from the oven and cool 5 minutes.

Place serving plate on top of the pie, invert plate and carefully remove pie plate. Serve warm. It tastes great with ice cream!

Pastry for 10-inch Double Crust

2 C. sifted flour
2/3 C. lard or shortening

1 tsp. salt
5-7 T. cold water

Sift flour and salt together. Cut in shortening with two knives or pastry cutter until pieces are the size of small peas.

Sprinkle 1 T. water over part of the mixture. Gently toss with fork, then push to the side of the bowl. Repeat until all is moistened. Form into 2 balls. Flatten on lightly floured surface. Wrap in foil. Refrigerate until ready to use.

Mose Annie's Sour Cream Apple Pie

2 T. flour	3/4 C. sugar
1/8 tsp. salt	1 egg
1 C. sour cream	1/2 tsp. vanilla
2 C. finely chopped apples	

Sift dry ingredients together. Add cream, egg & vanilla. Beat until smooth. Add apples. Mix well. Pour into pastry-lined pie pan.

Bake in a 400-degree oven for 10 minutes.   The bake in a350-degree oven for 30 minutes.

Topping:

1/3 C. sugar	1 tsp. cinnamon
1/3 C. butter	1/4 C. flour

Combine ingredients and mix thoroughly. Sprinkle over pie and return to oven. Bake at 400 degrees for 10 minutes.

Now this is just getting odder and odder. I was in town again. And again I saw Cousin Emma talking with Caleb Miller. I don't understand. What is going on? I have a strange feeling about this.

The whole time we were growing up, they didn't get along. They weren't exactly enemies, but they weren't friends, either. Caleb spent most of his time playing tricks on Cousin Emma. Besides the frog in church, he once left her a bucket of worms on her doorstep.

I saw him put them there myself. I was on my way over to play with Cousin Emma. I was still far enough away that Caleb didn't see me before I ducked behind a tree. He left the bucket on her front step.

When he was gone, I ran up to see what was inside. It was a bucket of worms. There was a note inside. It read, "For Emma. It takes one to know one." I was furious, but when I told Cousin Emma what I saw, she just shrugged her shoulders and said, "Well they'll be just fine for fishing." We went fishing that very afternoon. It was the beginning of Emma's lifelong passion for fishing. She drug me along every chance she got, since none of her brothers would go with her. She still fishes to this day.

Wait a minute. When I saw the two of them talking, they were holding something — fishing poles! And a bucket. Later I saw Caleb Miller's buggy parked down by the lake, the one that's considered the best fishing hole in the county.

Grandma Yoder's Apple Pie

Pastry for a double crust 9-inch pie   1/4 C. sugar
6 apples, peeled, cored & thinly sliced
1 tsp. vanilla extract   2 T. flour
1/2 tsp. cinnamon   1/4 tsp. ground ginger
1/8 tsp. ground mace   2 T. butter
Cream or whole milk

Heat oven to 425 degrees. Line a 9-inch pan with half the pastry. In a large bowl combine apples, sugar, flour, vanilla, cinnamon, ginger & mace. Blend well. Pour apple mixture into pastry-lined pie pan. Dot with butter.

Cover apple filling with the remaining pastry. Pinch together edges of bottom and top crusts to seal.

Brush the top crust with cream or milk. Cut slits in crust to vent steam.

Bake 20 minutes. reduce oven to 375 degrees and bake 30 to 35 minutes or until the apples are tender.

Apple Desserts

Magdalena's Applesauce Rolls.........................151
Suzanne's Applesauce 152
Mother's Favorite Apple Kuchen...................153
Apple Slices..155
Sarah's Chopped Apple Dessert......................157
Esther's Apple Dessert...................................159
Apple Crackle...161
Apple-Cake Dessert......................................162
Apple Bread Pudding.....................................165
Esther's Apple Kuchen...................................167

Magdalena's Applesauce Roll

2 C. flour	4 tsp. baking powder
1 tsp. salt	4 T. shortening
3/4 C. milk	

Sift dry ingredients. Cut in shortening. Add milk. Roll out. Spread with sweetened, thick applesauce. Roll up.

Melt 1/4 C. butter in pan which is at least 2" deep. Cut roll into slices and place cut side down in pan. Pour over the boiling syrup (1 C. sugar, 1 C. water, 1 tsp. vanilla boiled together 5 minutes). Bake in 450 degree oven for 20 minutes.

Suzanne's Applesauce

4 apples
1 T. cinnamon candy
3 large T. sugar

Peel and core apples. Section them into 4 pieces. Cook all the ingredients over a medium heat until apples are soft and the cinnamon candy and sugar are dissolved. Mash with a potato masher. Serve warm.

Mother's Favorite Apple Kuchen

1 C. flour	1/4 tsp. salt
2 T. sugar	1/2 C. butter

Mix with pastry cutter and pat in coffee cake pan. Peel and slice 4 C. apples. Add 1/2 C. sugar & 1/2 tsp. cinnamon. (More sugar is needed for some apples.) Mix and spread in crust.

Cover with streusel:

1/2 C. sifted flour	1/4 tsp. salt
4 T. butter	1/2 C. sugar

Bake 45-50 minutes in 350-degree oven.

My mother is by far the best all around cook I know. Many family members and friends have their specialties, but Mother is good at everything. In all the years I've known her, Mother has never had a failure behind the stove.

I've had my share. I should learn not to try a new recipe when company's coming. Most of the time the food has turned out just great, but not always. Luckily, my one big disaster was witnessed by just Cousin Emma. She came over early for a family gathering and saved the day when a potato casserole burnt. She whipped up mashed potatoes in record time and also took a broom and "swept" out that terrible burnt smell. No one was the wiser.

Apples Slices

2 C. sifted flour	1 tsp. sugar
2/3 C. shortening	1/2 C. milk
1 egg yolk, slightly beaten	2 T. flour
5 C. peeled, cored, sliced apples	1 1/2 C. sugar
1 egg white, slightly beaten	1 T. butter

Sift flour with salt. Cut in shortening until mixture resembles coarse crumbs. Mix egg yolk with milk and stir into flour mixture.

Pat half the dough into an 11 1/2x7x1 1/2" pan.

155

(continued)

Cover with apples. Mix the 2 T. flour with sugar. Sprinkle over apples. Dot with butter.

Roll the rest of the dough to fit into the pan. Place over apples. Brush with egg white. Bake 45 minutes at 375 degrees.

Cool slightly. Frost with powdered sugar frosting.

Sarah's Chopped Apple Dessert

1 egg	1 C. sugar
1 C. flour	2 tsp. baking powder
1/2 tsp. salt	4 tart apples
2 T. softened shortening	1 tsp. vanilla
1/2 C. chopped walnuts	

Beat egg. Add sugar, flour, baking powder and salt, which have been sifted together. Peel and cube apples. Add to the mixture. Stir thoroughly. Add shortening, vanilla and nuts. Bake in a 9x9-inch pan at 375 degrees for 30 minutes. Serve warm with whipped cream.

Our neighbors have a dog. They didn't want a dog. She showed up one day, as if she had a special invitation. Sarah stepped outside to call her family to supper. The dog sat down by the front door. She'd obviously been on her own for a long time. Her hair was matted. She had a lean, hungry look. But she also had another one that said, "I'm here, family." They named the dog "Apple." Why? Aaron, their youngest child, slipped Apple some of Sarah's Chopped Apple Dessert that first night. That's quite a sacrifice for an eight year old, especially since Sarah's dessert is so scrumptious. After that, Apple was just part of the family. She supervises the barn and keeps the other animals in line. And once in a great while, she gets to taste the dessert she's named after.

Esther's Apple Dessert

3 C. diced apples	1 1/2 tsp. soda
1 1/2 C. sugar	2 1/4 tsp. cinnamon
2 eggs, beaten	3/4 C. chopped nuts
1 1/2 C. flour	

Mix all ingredients together. Pour into a 9x9-inch baking pan. Bake at 350 degrees for 35 minutes. While cake is baking, mix together in a pan to cook on top of stove:

3/4 C. brown sugar	3 T. flour
1/2 C. sugar	1 1/2 C. water

(continued)

Boil until smooth and thick. Remove from the heat and add 1/4 C. butter and 1 1/2 tsp. vanilla. Stir well and pour over hot cake. Let cool. Before serving, cut into squares and serve with whipped topping.

Apple Crackle

2 eggs, beaten	**1/2 C. chopped walnuts**
3/4 C. sugar	**1 tsp. vanilla**
1/2 C. flour	**1 C. diced apples**
1 1/2 tsp. baking powder	**1/2 tsp. almond extract**
1/2 tsp. salt	

Add sugar to eggs and beat well. Sift flour, baking powder and salt. Add to egg mixture. Add walnuts, vanilla, apples and almond extract. Pour into 9-inch pie pan. Bake at 350 degrees for 30-45 minutes. Serve with whipped cream or ice cream.

Apple-Cake Dessert

1 C. flour
2 1/2 oz. softened butter
3/4 C. + 3 T. sugar
1 3/4 tsp. cinnamon, divided
1 lb. firm, tart apples (2 C.)

1 tsp. baking powder
1/4 tsp. baking soda
Pinch of salt
3 eggs
whipped cream

Preheat oven to 350. Grease 13x9x2-inch pan. Combine flour, baking powder and soda, salt & 1 tsp. cinnamon. Mix well. Set aside. Peel, core & chop apples. Stir flour mixture into butter mixture. Fold in apples. Spread dough in pan. Mix remaining 3 T. sugar and 3/4 tsp. cinnamon. Sprinkle over batter. Bake 30 minutes. Serve warm or cooled with whipped topping.

I was visiting Cousin Emma the other day. We don't live very far apart. Son Ethan and Husband David was in town at the hardware store. I had all my chores done. I'd baked some of my apple cookies. These are Cousin Emma's favorite cookie. So, I thought I'd walk over and surprise her. I was the one who got the surprise.

Cousin Emma was sitting in the front room, with the door wide open. I got an overwhelming smell of something sweet. Out of the corner of my eye, I saw a splash of color. Flowers in a fruit jar. How nice. Cousin Emma was humming something to herself. I don't think it was a hymn. At least it wasn't one I'm familiar with. I knocked on the door jam with my free hand. It wasn't until then that Cousin

Emma even noticed me. She smiled and asked me in. Something was different.

"Are you working on a new quilt, Cousin Emma?"

She just smiled and nodded. I looked at the beautiful flowers. They weren't any from her garden. They were store bought. Fancy. I know that Cousin Emma would never buy herself flowers. How ridiculous. I noticed a little white card on the table beside them. A gift? Then I saw the quilt. It was a double ring wedding quilt.

"Who's getting married, Cousin Emma?" She just smiled, pointing to herself. I dropped the plate of cookies.

Apple Bread Pudding

2 apples, peeled & sliced	2 eggs
2 C. day-old cubed bread	1/2 C. sugar
4 C. scalded milk	1/2 tsp. salt
1 tsp. vanilla	1/2 C. butter, melted
1/2 C. chopped walnuts	1/2 C. raisins

Place cubed bread in a bowl. Pour scalded milk over the bread until well soaked and slightly cooled. Beat eggs until mixed. Add sugar, salt and vanilla to the eggs. Stir into the bread mixture. Add melted butter and stir.

(continued)

Grease a 2-quart baking dish. Pour the pudding into the dish. Add apples, walnuts and raisins. Stir together. Set dish in a pan containing 1 inch hot water. Bake in a 350-degree oven for 60 to 75 minutes or when a knife inserted in the middle is not too wet.

Esther's Apple Kuchen

Dough:

2 T. butter	
1/4 C. sugar	
1 tsp. baking powder	

1 egg plus milk to fill 1/2 C.	
1 1/4 C. flour	
1/2 tsp. salt	

Mix dry ingredients. Add shortening. Beat egg slightly and add milk. Combine the two mixtures. Roll or pat 1/4" thick in the coffee cake pan.

Slice, peel and core apples. Mix with 1/2 C. sugar, 1 T. flour. Place apples and mixture on dough.

(continued)

Cover with the following custard:

Beat 1 egg, 1/2 C. sugar and 2 T. cream. Sprinkle with cinnamon.

Bake for 15 minutes at 350 degrees. reduce oven to 325 degrees. Bake another 15 or 20 minutes.

stood there. Just past the threshold of Jacob's house. The House Cousin Emma lived in all her life. The one her parents built. The one where she was born. The house with the Crossdawdy (Grandfather's house) where Emma's parents now live, since they retired from farming and turned over the operation to Jacob.

"Cousin Emma? Who?" It's all I could get out. I stared at her, waiting for the answer.

"Who are you going to marry? Who? After all these years? Who?"

"The man who asked me to go fishing."

"What? Who?" We were speaking the same language, but what was she saying?

"Oh, Cousin Kathy!" She laughed out loud. Her face was red. "You know, Cousin Kathy. You've got to know."

Slowly the candle light in my brain started to flicker. It turned into a bright flame. And then, a forest fire. "Caleb Miller?"

Cousin Emma smiled, nodding her head up and down. "He asked me to go fishing with him for the rest of my life."

I grabbed Cousin Emma and we hugged, forgetting the broken plate and the cookies.

NEED GIFTS?

Are you up a stump for some nice gifts for some nice people in your life? Here's a list of some great cookbooks. Just check 'em off, stick a check in an envelope with these pages, and we'll get your books off to you. Add $3.50 for shipping and handling for the first book and then $.50 cents more for each additional one. If you order over $50.00, forget the shipping and handling.

$5.95 Mini Cookbooks
(Only 3 1/2 x 5) With Maxi Good Eatin' - 160 or 176 pages - $5.95

- ☐ Alabama Cooking
- ☐ Arkansas Cooking
- ☐ Dixie Cooking
- ☐ Georgia Cooking
- ☐ Illinois Cooking
- ☐ Indiana Cooking
- ☐ Iowa Cookin'
- ☐ Kansas Cookin'
- ☐ Massachusetts Cooking
- ☐ Missouri Cookin'
- ☐ Minnesota Cookin'
- ☐ New Hampshire Cooking
- ☐ New Jersey Cooking
- ☐ New Mexico Cooking
- ☐ New York Cooking
- ☐ North Carolina Cooking
- ☐ Off To College Cookbook
- ☐ Ohio Cooking
- ☐ Pennsylvania Cooking
- ☐ South Carolina Cooking
- ☐ Tennessee Cooking

- ☐ Cooking with Things Go Splash
- ☐ Virginia Cooking
- ☐ Wisconsin Cooking
- ☐ Amish-Mennonite Peach Cookbook
- ☐ Amish & Mennonite Strawberry Cookbook
- ☐ Apples Galore
- ☐ Blueberry Blues Cookbook
- ☐ Bountiful Blueberries
- ☐ Citrus! Citrus! Citrus!
- ☐ Cooking Seafood & Poultry with Wine
- ☐ Cooking with Asparagus
- ☐ Cooking with Cider
- ☐ Cooking with Garlic
- ☐ Cooking with Spirits
- ☐ Cooking with Sweet Onions
- ☐ Cooking with Wine
- ☐ Cooking with Things Go Baa
- ☐ Cooking with Things Go Cluck
- ☐ Cooking with Things Go Moo
- ☐ Cooking with Things Go Oink

- ☐ Working Girl Cookbook
- ☐ To Take the *Gamey* out of the Game Cookbook
- ☐ Super Simple Cookin'
- ☐ Some Like It Hot
- ☐ Recipes for Desserts Using Wine
- ☐ Using Wine
- ☐ Recipes for Appetizers & Beverages
- ☐ Pumpkins! Pumpkins! Pumpkins!
- ☐ Nuts! Nuts! Nuts!
- ☐ Muffins Cookbook (Veggies, Fruit, Nut)
- ☐ Midwest Small Town Cookin'
- ☐ Kid Pumpkin Fun Book
- ☐ Kid Money
- ☐ Kid Cookin'
- ☐ Great New England Cookbook
- ☐ Good Cookin' From the Plain People
- ☐ Dixie Cookbook
- ☐ Crazy for Basil
- ☐ CSA Cookbook ($4.95)

$6.95 Mini Cookbooks
176 - 204 pages - $6.95

- ❏ Arizona Cooking
- ❏ Dakota Cooking
- ❏ Kentucky Cookin'
- ❏ Southwest Cooking
- ❏ Amish-Mennonite Apple Cookbook
- ❏ Amish-Mennonite Berry Cookbook
- ❏ Amish-Mennonite Pumpkin Cookbook
- ❏ Apples! Apples! Apples!
- ❏ Berries! Berries! Berries!
- ❏ Berries Galore
- ❏ Cherries Galore
- ❏ Cooking Greens Southern Style
- ❏ Cooking with Mulling Spices
- ❏ Crockpot Cookbook
- ❏ Grass-Fed Beef Recipes
- ❏ The Grilling & BBQ Cookbook
- ❏ Holiday & Get-Together Cookbook
- ❏ Herbs! Herbs! Herbs!
- ❏ How to Make Salsa
- ❏ Peaches! Peaches! Peaches!
- ❏ Pecans! Pecans! Pecans!
- ❏ Renaissance Cokery Book
- ❏ Soup's On!

($6.95 continued)

- ❏ Veggie Talk Coloring & Story Book
- ❏ Winter Squash Cookbook
- ❏ The Zero Calorie Chocolate Cookbook

In-Between Cookbooks
(5 1/2 x 8 1/2) - 150 pages - $9.95

- ❏ Adaptable Apple Cookbook
- ❏ Amish Ladies Cookbook - Old Husbands
- ❏ Amish Ladies Cookbook - Young Husbands
- ❏ Amish Ladies Carry-To-The-Field Cold Lunches Cookbook
- ❏ An Apple A Day Cookbook
- ❏ Baseball Moms' Cookbook
- ❏ Basketball Moms' Cookbook
- ❏ Bird Up! Pheasant Cookbook
- ❏ Buffalo Cookbook
- ❏ Camp Cookin'
- ❏ Catfish Cookin' Cookbook
- ❏ Civil War Cookin', Stories, 'n Such
- ❏ Cherokee Native American Book of Recipes
- ❏ Cooking Ala Nude
- ❏ Cooking for a Crowd
- ❏ Cooking Up Some Winners Cookbook

($9.95 continued)

- ❏ Cooking with Beer
- ❏ Cooking with Moonshine
- ❏ Country Cooking
  Recipes from my Amish Heritage
- ❏ Das Hausbarn Cookbook
- ❏ Eating Ohio
- ❏ Farmers Market Cookbook
- ❏ Feast of Moons Indian Cookbook
- ❏ Funky Duck Cookbook
- ❏ Halloween Fun Book
- ❏ Hunting in the Nude Cookbook
- ❏ Indian Cooking Cookbook
- ❏ Japanese Cooking
- ❏ Keep The Skinny Kid Skinny Cookbook
- ❏ Kids' No-Cook Cookbook
- ❏ Mad About Garlic
- ❏ Market to Kitchen
- ❏ Mormon Trail Cookbook
- ❏ New Cooks' Cookbook
- ❏ No-Stove, No-Sharp Knife Kids' Cookbook
- ❏ Norwegian Cooking
- ❏ Off the Farm, Out of the Garden Cookbook
- ❏ Outdoor Cooking for Outdoor Men
- ❏ Plantation Cookin' Cookbook
- ❏ Pumpkin Patch, Proverbs & Pies

HEARTS 'N TUMMIES COOKBOOK CO.
3544 Blakslee St. • Wever, Iowa 52658
1-800-571-2665

Name _____

Address _____

Ph.# _____

*You Iowa folks gotta kick in another 6% for Sales Tax.

($9.95 continued)
- ☐ Shhh Cookbook
- ☐ Soccer Mom's Cookbook
- ☐ Southwest Native American Cookbook
- ☐ Southwest Vegetarian Cookbook
- ☐ Trailer Trash Cookbook
- ☐ Vegan Vegetarian Cookbook
- ☐ Venison Cookbook
- ☐ Vittles Fixin's Cookbook
- ☐ Western Frontier Cookbook

Biggie Cookbooks
(5 1/2 x 8 1/2) - 200 plus pages - $11.95
- ☐ Aphrodisiac Cooking
- ☐ Barn Raising & Threshers Cookbook

($11.95 continued)
- ☐ Buy Fresh, Buy Local Cookbook
- ☐ Chesapeake Bay Cookbook
- ☐ Dial-a-Dream Cookbook
- ☐ Covered Bridges Cookbook
- ☐ Depression Times Cookbook
- ☐ Discover the Philippines Cookbook
- ☐ Diva Cooking
- ☐ Flat Out, Dirt Cheap Cookin'
- ☐ Grandma's Cookbook
- ☐ Grits Shall Rise Again
- ☐ Have You Considered Cooking
- ☐ High-Fiber Cookbook
- ☐ Hormone Helper Cookbook
- ☐ I-Got-Funner-Things-To Do
- ☐ Le Ricette (Italian) Cookbook

($11.95 continued)
- ☐ Lumber Camp & Saw Milling Cookbook
- ☐ Mississippi River Cookbook
- ☐ Quilters' Cookbook
- ☐ Real Men Cook on Sunday Cookbook
- ☐ Southern Homemade Cooking
- ☐ Spice 'N Wine Cookbook
- ☐ Taste of Las Vegas Cookbook
- ☐ Vegetarian Wild Game Cookbook
- ☐ Victorian Sunday Dinners
- ☐ Wild Critter Cookbook

Even Bigger Cookbooks
- ☐ Body Shop ($14.95)
- ☐ Food Preservation A-Z ($14.95)
- ☐ Passion for Peaches ($13.00)